Within the Lines of Tarot

By

MANIFEST

REALITY

Glossary

Journey of The Way

With this book, you are given a formal introduction to the patterns of force and form recognized in progression of life. The manifest form of archetypal-macro-expressions. As you progress, through the Tarot, you will attract a deeper level of self understanding as you engage.

Tarot, is a deeply spiritual tool of profound psychological significance. Originating from Egyptian depictions of history and myth, introduced into Europe in the 14th century.

400 years later, the truth of it's origin was discovered. Not long after this discovery, many people began devoting their efforts toward unlocking the secrets of Tarot.

In Kabbalah, the esoteric form of Abrahamic Religion, The 22 Major Arcana were discovered to be correspondent with the pathways connecting Sephirot to the Tree of Life.

The Fool cannot skip any roads, nor can he get stuck. He must 'understand' each of the 22 Major Arcana, for his mission is to complete it and return home.

The pathways provide the frame for the Tree of Life, as such, the premise of Tarot can easily be understood as The Fool's Journey of The Way.

Like all forms of energy, The Fool begins as mere potential and raw energy before he can take form to realize his full potential.

From the moment of his emanation from the Source, he sets forth on a personal quest of individuation and self definition. He must follow the way to find his passion and so begins, the Major Arcana, The greater mysteries on our Journey of The Way.

Enjoy.

— Jacob L. Castle

Major Arcana

0 – The Fool

Spirit of The Ether. The Fool draws intimations of purity of being and transformation. The Sun is at his back and his belongings are as an extension of his self, as he is of the Sun. The Fool is the totality of the Godhead dwelling in Christ as the familiar extension of existential relation. He is the reality of being within the familiar relationship of family and express communication of implication to the affect of all.

Upright

Ideas, Spontaneity, Adventure, Potential, Originality, Purity, Being Present, Sensitivity

_____

_____

_____

_____

Reverse

Indecision, Folly, Gullibility, Naivety, Boredom, Stationary, Hesitation, Mental Oedipism

_____

_____

_____

_____

Notes

_____

_____

_____

_____

_____

_____

_____

_____

O

THE FOOL.

1 – The Magician

Magus of Power. The Magician, through action and will, is the spiritual bridge. Framed beneath the image of the infinite, The Magician wears the belt of Ouroboros around his waist. Corresponding with the totality of his being the archetypal vessel of serpent bearing vessels. Upon his table are the correspondents to being, the physicality of earth, receptivity of water, mentality of air, and extension of fire.

Upright

Creativity, Action, Manifestation, Skill, Wisdom, Adaptation, Concentration, Confidence

_____
_____
_____
_____

Reverse

Deceit, Unease, Communication Block, Abuse of Power, Powerlessness, Arrogance

_____
_____
_____
_____

Notes

_____
_____
_____
_____
_____
_____
_____

2 – The High Priestess

Priestess of The Silver Star. The High Priestess, eternal virgin clothed in feminine light, shields her heart with a cross and upon her lap the Law is revealed. The High Priestess, is sandwiched between the pillars of mercy and severity, her communication is subtle, reflected by the Moon at her feet. Upon her head is the solar disk supported by cow horns, correspondent to Isis, queen of the throne.

Upright

Subconscious Connection, Intuition, Hidden Light, Anima, Discovery of Truth

Reverse

Ignorance, Shortsightedness, Misusing Spirituality, Misusing Intuition, Misusing Beauty

Notes

3 – The Empress

Great Mother and Daughter of The Mighty Ones. The Empress is the divine aspect which nurtures and consumes; manifestation of creation framed in the image of being as the form complimentary to force. Upon her head is a crown of seven stars and beneath her seat is a shield, emblazoned with the mark of Venus. The Empress is the invitation to reconnect with the natural formality of the world to engage with life in a manner that facilitates and nourishes benevolent creation.

Upright

Happiness, Success, Action, Nurturer, Abundance, Fertility, Creation, Creative Resolution

_____
_____
_____
_____

Reverse

Disconnection, Stagnation, Wastefulness, Lack of Interest, Inaction, Infertility, Neglect

_____
_____
_____
_____

Notes

_____
_____
_____
_____
_____
_____
_____

4 – The Emperor

Great Father and Son of the Morning. The Emperor, seated upon his concrete throne, holds a sphere in one hand and a cane in the shape of an ankh in the other, correspondent with reality and rebirth. He is the masculine energy that manifests order, providing information to the ordering principle. He soothes the raging sea and upholds the law as the leading figure, assuring the protection of his bride.

Upright

Authority, Law, Power, Structure, Paternal Energy, Rationale, Stability, Sovereignty, Animus

_____

_____

_____

_____

Reverse

Weakness, Cruelty, Rigidity, Ineffectiveness, Lawlessness, Fragility, Powerlessness

_____

_____

_____

_____

Notes

_____

_____

_____

_____

_____

_____

_____

5 – The Hierophant

Magus of the Eternal Gods. The Hierophant is guardian and interpreter of the governing order. Well versed in the principle of the image, he interprets wisdom and formality through knowledge of the consensual image with which the subject was originally produced. In his left hand, he holds the triple cross, indicative of the three aeons of Isis, Osiris, and Horus; and with his right hand, he signals divine wisdom.

Upright

Spiritual Guidance, Institutional Application, Divine Wisdom, Learning, Divine Order

_____

_____

_____

_____

Reverse

Group Identifixations, Unorthodox Occultation, Idolatry, Zealotry, Dogmatists

_____

_____

_____

_____

Notes

THE HIEROPHANT.

6 – The Lovers

Children of the Voice Divine. The Lovers are the justice of union, duality, and attraction. The Lovers signify the eternal force of marriage, the natural order creating the holy union. Whether it is a relationship, an event, personal decision, or idea; The Lovers manifest to ask that decisions be made in open communication with the soul, the true self of motivation.

Upright

Inspiration, Beauty, Choices, Love, Engagement, Action, Unification, Relationship, Trust

_____

_____

_____

_____

Reverse

Infidelity, Failure to Test, Disconnection, Relationship Issues, Imbalance

_____

_____

_____

_____

Notes

_____

_____

_____

_____

_____

_____

_____

_____

7 – The Chariot

Lord of Triumph. The Chariot is the force of a unified totality, manifest in willpower, determination, and self-understanding. When aimed at subduing the dividing forces of chaos, The Chariot is pulled by the self-discipline found in equilibrium with Love and Power. Covering his chariot is the midnight veil of stars. Still, he projects justified confidence; correspondent with his wand held upright and his crown of sacred and divine significance.

Upright

Drive, Will-Power, Perseverance, Health, Voyage, Ambition, Victory, Triumph, Direction

_____
_____
_____
_____

Reverse

Scattered Energy, Defeat, Aggression, Detours, Loss of Will, Off-Railing, Self-Doubt

_____
_____
_____
_____

Notes

_____
_____
_____
_____
_____
_____
_____
_____

THE CHARIOT.

8 – Strength

Daughter of the Flaming Sword. Strength is mastery of the lower by the higher. The joy of Strength is shown in her complete ease and self-awareness, shown in her capacity for disciplined submission. Above her head, the sign of infinity shines, reminding us of the true power. Through patience, lovingkindness, and compassion the lion assumes the balance of control, a feat only Strength can provide.

Upright

Strength, Courage, Power, Self-Assurance, Self-Control, Potency, Compassion, Will-Power

_____

_____

_____

_____

Reverse

Little Courage, Doubt, Pettiness, Impotence, Sickness, Vanity, Hedonism, Struggle, Pride, Rage

_____

_____

_____

_____

Notes

_____

_____

_____

_____

_____

_____

_____

_____

STRENGTH.

9 – The Hermit

Magus of the Voice of Light. The Hermit holds up the sacred lantern of sacred and divine union, offering passage through even the densest fog. In his left hand, the Hermit holds a staff from which his head rests upon in prayer. Advising us to reflect upon our self, looking inward for truth and wisdom as you are your best guide. Be mindful and calm as you reflect on the life giving waters of the sea, for their reflection corresponds with you.

Upright

Self-Reflection, Divine Inspiration, Enlightenment, Meditation, Selfless Oneness

_____

_____

_____

_____

Reverse

Withdrawal, Rashness, Isolation, Self-Absorption, Depression, Social Misfit, Exile

_____

_____

_____

_____

Notes

_____

_____

_____

_____

_____

_____

_____

_____

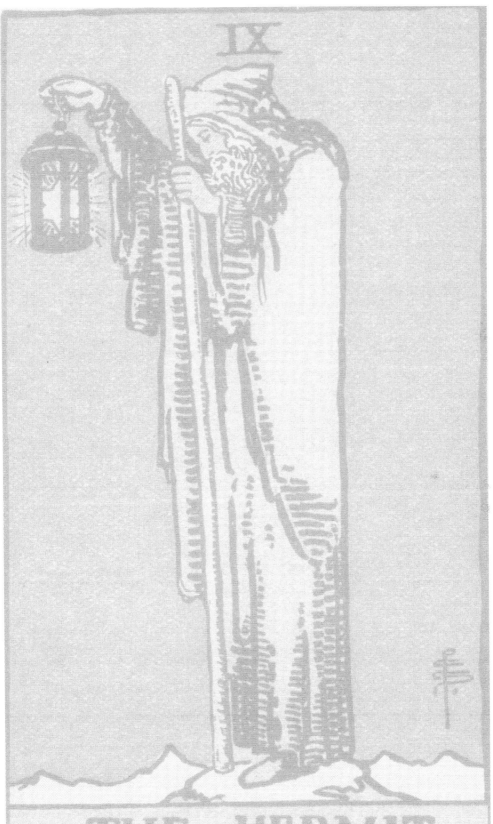

10 – Wheel of Fortune

Lord of The Forces of Life. The Wheel of Fortune bears the letters T, A, R, and O; clockwise reveals TARO, counterclockwise reveals TORA. Showing the perspective cyclical nature of archetypal significance. The four corners provide the Tetramorph, reflecting the divine force of elemental form; while in dualistic fashion, circling the wheel are the sacred forms of elemental force reflected in progression of the Serpent, Seth, and Sphinx.

Upright

Luck, Chance, Opportunity, Cycles of Life, Good Fortune, Happiness, Success, Changes

_____

_____

_____

_____

Reverse

Misfortune, Mishaps, Resistance, Failure, Broken Sequence, Disappointments, Setbacks

_____

_____

_____

_____

Notes

11 – Justice

Daughter of the Lord of Truth. Justice is the karmic retribution revealing the truth of intent, the truth of intent shown from decisions made prior. Justice shows that present action influences future circumstance, if the truth revealed in the past is made conscious, that is. In her left hand she holds the divine scales and in her right hand she wields the sword of truth. Revealing her capacity for understanding and wisdom to see through illusion, through to the heart of ignorance.

Upright

Karma, Truth, Balance, Alignment, Divine Significance of Sacred Responsibility

_____
_____
_____
_____

Reverse

Corruption, Miscarriage of Justice, Bias, False Accusations, Dispute, Hypocrisy

_____
_____
_____
_____

Notes

_____
_____
_____
_____
_____
_____
_____

XI

JUSTICE .

12 – The Hanged Man

Spirit of The Mighty Waters. The Hanged Man, suspended with a rope secured to his heel, is enlightened by his decision to hang. Just as the young boy is exalted to become a man in respect of responsibility. The Hanged Man is the realization invoking new order to be reborn, rejuvenating the truth of wisdom with resolve. The Hanged Man is correspondent to the crosses we responsibly choose to bare.

Upright

Letting Go, Sacrifice, New Perspective, Surrender, Breaking Patterns, Metamorphosis

_____
_____
_____
_____

Reverse

Missing Opportunities, In Limbo, False Prophecy, Delusion, Indecision, False Motives

_____
_____
_____
_____

Notes

_____
_____
_____
_____
_____
_____
_____

13 – Death

Child of the Great Transformers and Harbinger of Retribution. Death, the skeletal figure sitting upon her horse as the lone survivor, defying the constraints of time and resentment of nature. Death is the shroud which endures the forge, the relinquishing of illusion, and shedding of the decaying husk. Death is giving up the old and familiar to make way for the unfamiliar and new, breaking the habits and addictions to forge a new relationship with existence. Death is revelation.

Upright

Profound Change, Beginnings, Transitions, End of Era's, Renewal, Rebirth, New Aion

_____
_____
_____
_____

Reverse

Delayed Endings, Holding on to the Past, Resistance, Stagnation, Going through the Motions

_____
_____
_____
_____

Notes

_____
_____
_____
_____
_____
_____
_____
_____

DEATH.

14 – Temperance

Daughter of the Reconcilers and fulfillment of the Lovers. Temperance is the balance of opposing forces and Angel of sacred wisdom, encouraging harmony between extremes. Temperance, with one foot in the water and another on land, shows; just as water flows from one cup to another, being is one and of the same, flowing between differing states of perspective awareness, influencing the flow of extremes within contextual reality.

Upright

Harmony, Balance, Synthesis, Moderation, Blending, Synergy, Alchemy, Blending of Opposites

_____
_____
_____
_____

Reverse

Imbalance, Lacking Patience, Anger, Excess, Frustration, Misapplication of Wisdom

_____
_____
_____
_____

Notes

_____
_____
_____
_____
_____
_____
_____
_____

XIV

TEMPERANCE.

15 – The Devil

Lord of the Gates of Matter and Son of the Serpent's Kiss. Beneath him is nakedness of man and woman. The Devil lights the tails of shackled men ablaze; while, the shackled woman stands pointing to her fruit. This is the layering of reason, concealing the sacred truth of divine relationship. It is the loose shackles of a divided and unholy mindset believing in the disconnection of reality.

Upright

Bondage, Temptation, Addiction, Fear, Obsession, Denial, Challenges, Deceit, Illusion

_____

_____

_____

_____

Reverse

Detachment, Breakthrough, Vulnerability, Awareness, Acknowledging Life

_____

_____

_____

_____

Notes

_____

_____

_____

_____

_____

_____

_____

_____

THE DEVIL .

16 – The Tower

Lord of the Hosts of the Mighty. The Tower appears when the preferred illusion encounters the truth of reality ignored. The Tower is correspondent to removing the false crown of illusion, exposing oneself to the vulnerability of truth to allow yourself to be seen for who you are. The familiar breakdown and arrival of discomfort is sacred reflection to divine pain of reality's rejection.

Upright

Sudden and Unexpected Change, Destruction, Ruin, Rude Awakenings, Revelation

_____
_____
_____
_____

Reverse

Prolonged Upheaval, Disruption, Denial, Resistance to Change, Blockages Removed

_____
_____
_____
_____

Notes

_____
_____
_____
_____
_____
_____
_____
_____

THE TOWER.

17 – The Star

Daughter of the Firmament, Shining Light of the Guiding Principle, and Fulfillment of The Soul. The Star is the light shining brightest when entering new phases of life to remind you of presence. The Star reminds us of our connection to the universe by informing us of the available wisdom within. The Star's light is near to show you the time to embrace new ideas and growth, but be aware of reflections of that matter; for the light of the Lover is the clothing of Stars, who are in light of the Sun.

Upright

Hope, Happiness, Opportunities, Optimism, Renewal, Serenity, Spirituality, Beauty, Clarity

_____

_____

_____

_____

Reverse

Confusion, Disappointment, Spiritual Blockages, Figures of Contempt, Addiction

_____

_____

_____

_____

Notes

_____

_____

_____

_____

_____

_____

_____

18 – The Moon

Ruler of the Flux and Reflux, Partner in Reflection to the Sun, and brightest light in the night sky. The Moon appears as the transference of alchemical forces which accrue throughout the day. The Moon can appear as a blanket of illusion separating you from reality. But, by overcoming fear, exposing yourself to the shadow by expanding your awareness of ignorance, the soft radiant glow becomes the soothing truth to be received and integrated by the shadow of the unknown.

Upright

Intuition, Dreams, Hidden Things, Fear, Subconscious, Emotions, Reflection

_____

_____

_____

_____

Reverse

Secrets Revealed, Deception Seen, Revelation, Unhappiness, Frustration, Illusion

_____

_____

_____

_____

Notes

_____

_____

_____

_____

_____

_____

_____

19 – The Sun

Lord of the Fire of The World and Lord of the New Aion. The Sun is the truth of extension and beneficent source of life, melting away the wax to provide the truth in the light of a burning candle. The Sun appears to usher an end of the night, shining down confidence and awakening. The Sun is the all in all and all in the all, familiarity of relationship, and intercontextual significance of relationship,

Upright

Life, Energy, Vitality, Joy, Optimism, Enlightenment, Clarity, Lovingkindness

_____

_____

_____

_____

Reverse

Partial Success, Illusion, Conceit, Selfishness, Egotism, Depression, Narcissism, Isolationism

_____

_____

_____

_____

Notes

_____

_____

_____

_____

_____

_____

_____

_____

20 – Judgment

Spirit of the Primal Fire. Judgment, above the clouds, smiles from on high. Below her angel, the people rise from their graves, to relinquish their suffering and be reborn. Judgment appears when it is time for self-evaluation. It is the crux for new life and its fire must be accepted to purge that which no longer serves. This is the card following in the wake of your shadow made known. It is the retribution of earth as the trumpet is blown by her angels, the implications of intent returned to sender.

Upright

Redemption, Rebirth, Awakening, Realization, Rite of Passage, Moving On, Reunion

_____

_____

_____

_____

Reverse

Self-Doubt, Stagnation, Delayed Change, Decision Avoidance, Shadow Work Required

_____

_____

_____

_____

Notes

_____

_____

_____

_____

_____

_____

21 – The World

Great One of the Night of Time. The World blossoms out from the tetramorphic forces, unfurling like wings of embrace. The World is mind of god, the all in all, where all is in the all. Wreathed within the conscious awareness and acceptance of responsibility, The World is the microcosm within itself, it is the journey, bearing wands in left and right hands, and seeker of justified being. All in significant affect to birth the Holy Child.

Upright

Completion, Fulfillment, Possibilities, Realizations, Embracing Reality, Travel

_____
_____
_____
_____

Reverse

Regret, Doubt, Unfinished Business, Delayed Success, Stagnation, Incomplete

_____
_____
_____
_____

Notes

_____
_____
_____
_____
_____
_____
_____
_____

Minor Arcana

Royalty

Kings are the fire of the minor arcana, they are the projections of authority and power. The Kings are correspondent to what it takes to succeed.

Queens are the water of the minor arcana, they are the feminine significance of subconscious response. The Queens are correspondent to wisdom and stability.

Knights are the air of the minor arcana, they are all about vigor and growth. The Knights are correspondent to the knowing of where you're going, and telling you it's time to set your wheels in motion to achieve.

Pages are the earth of the minor arcana, they are the environment of messengers and beginnings of growth. The Pages are correspondent to insight into procedural awareness, allowing you to foresight before taking your next steps.

Numbers

Aces represent beginnings. They indicate initiative, drive, potential, and the earliest stages of an endeavor. They correspond with the manifestation of significance.

Twos carry messages of balance. They indicate the duality of dichotomy, equilibrium, and love. They correspond with the manifestation of vibration.

Threes are about communication, relationship, and interaction. They indicate the affluence of life, work, and emotions. Correspondent with fire, reason, and stability.

Fours represent a revelation in correspondence for a rest period. In order to move forward, you need to stop now and observe where you've been.

Fives deal with adversity. These are indicative of conflict, loss, and other negative experiences in your life that must be resolved.

Sixes represent growth, overcoming challenges, leaving bad situations behind, and gaining a greater understanding of who you are right now.

Sevens offer guidance and assurance. Urging that you must have faith in yourself and be responsible for the world.

Eights are about action and change. These cards tell you that the only way to get where you want to be is to change what you're doing right now.

Nines represent fruition. Things are coming together and you are beginning to attract the response of completion.

Tens are about final outcomes and the end of a current cycle. They carry messages about the rewards you experience for the work you invest.

Suit of Wands

Suit of Wands

The Suit of Wands are correspondent to the conscious insight at the core of who you are.

As Above, So Below.

The progression of the Wands tells the story of consciousness as the resolution of self becomes increasingly conscious. Their focus is on depicting explicit actions and implicit expressions, arising in pursuit of significance, meaning, and self understanding. They act as a guide through subconscious progression of actualizing potential energy, as the awareness of sacred masculine responsibility.

The Wands are correspondent to consciousness and fire; their direction is South; and their astral correspondence is Aries, Leo, and Sagittarius.

King of Wands

Prince of the Chariot of Fire. The King of Wands, fire of fire, depicts a king sitting upon a throne of lions and oroborean salamanders. His crown is fiery and his wand is grounded. The King of Wands is correspondent to the pure energy of the fiery masculine force. He is the visionary servant leader, delivering the results of action to lead with an intentional vision for a desired future; all while keeping the lives of others in the forefront of his mind.

Upright

Swiftness, Strength, Influence, Respect, Leadership, Maturity, Visionary, Honor

_____
_____
_____
_____

Reverse

Intolerant, Ruthless, Impatient, Impulsive, Prejudiced, Cruel, Austere, Autocratic

_____
_____
_____
_____

Notes

_____
_____
_____
_____
_____
_____
_____

KING of WANDS

Queen of Wands

Queen of the Thrones of Flame. Queen of Wands, water of fire, depicts a queen sitting upon a similar throne as the king; however, hers is decorated with sun flowers. Her crown is of the sun, as she hold both wand and sunflower in her hands. The Queen of Wands is correspondent to the upbeat, courageous, and determined nature of fire and strength within life. She is the divine voice calling for the concrete stability of the Emperor to be manifest while retaining the friendly nature of the Fool.

Upright

Courage, Confidence, Independence, Determination, Creativity, Intuition, Passion

_____

_____

_____

_____

Reverse

Shallow Self-Confidence, Re-Establish Sense of Self, Cold, Jealous, Domineering

_____

_____

_____

_____

Notes

QUEEN of WANDS.

Knight of Wands

Lord of Flames and Lightning. The Knight of Wands, air of fire, depicts a knight, decorated in salamanders, rearing up with his wand held high. The Knight of Wands corresponds with the mental force behind actions made in pursuit of the principle. Dressed in the flames of action, he reminds us to be of sure mind, to embolden and bolster our courage when facing the truth within the unknown expanse.

Upright

Energy, Passion, Inspired Action, Impulsiveness, Determination, Movement, Wit, Force

_____

_____

_____

_____

Reverse

Haste, Scattered Energy, Delays, Frustration, Egotism, Anger, Blockages, Misspent Creativity

_____

_____

_____

_____

Notes

_____

_____

_____

_____

_____

_____

_____

_____

KNIGHT of WANDS.

Page of Wands

Princess of the Shining Flame. The Page of Wands, earth of fire, depicts a princess, clothed in salamanders, beneath a cloak. Standing in admiration of her wand, she is the divine spark of motion, reality of being, and inclination to give your all in life. The Page of Wands is correspondent to the establishing of new and creative ideas. The creative energy of force to act upon form, grounding it with reality in the act of creation; planting the seed of passion, she is the impression received in our being.

Upright

Enthusiasm, Renewed Vigor, Faithfulness, Travel, Creativity, Exploration, Communication

_____
_____
_____
_____

Reverse

Superficiality, Theatrics, Cruelty, Instability, Gossip, Unfocused, Arrogance, Pessimism

_____
_____
_____
_____

Notes

_____
_____
_____
_____
_____
_____
_____

PAGE of WANDS.

Ace of Wands

Lord of the Root of the Powers of Fire. The Ace of Wands depicts a golden hand appearing from without the clouds of unconscious manifestation holding a wand sprouting leaves, correspondent to the phenomenality of extensive being. The Ace of Wands is the purity of realizing the Magician and Fool as one, marking the beginning stages of manifestation as the creation of potential opportunity relays the significance of being, as such. The Ace of Wands is the purity of reality.

Upright

Inspiration, Potential, Enthusiasm, Growth, New Opportunities, Vigor, Gain

_____
_____
_____
_____

Reverse

Endings, Delay, Impatience, False Starts, Cancellation, Emerging Ideas, Distractions, Lack of Focus

_____
_____
_____
_____

Notes

_____
_____
_____
_____
_____
_____
_____
_____

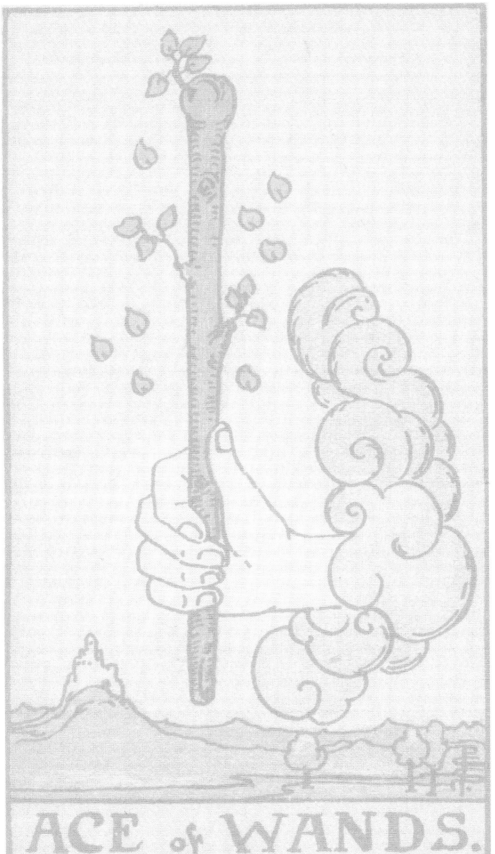

ACE of WANDS.

Two of Wands

Lord of Dominion. The Two of Wands depicts a man standing atop the lookout, leaning over the parapet, observing the expanse before him while, in his hand, rests the orb of the world; two wands are beside him, but the man holds onto the wand planted in cement. The Two of Wands corresponds to the reality of being in admiration of reality, the truth of perspective relevance coupled with the intercontext of being within the familiar illusion of independent relation.

Upright

Focus, Decisions, Discovery, Dominion, Harmonious Rule, Justice, Courage, Restlessness

_____

_____

_____

_____

Reverse

Turbulence, Sadness, Trouble, Overconfidence, Stunted, Undetermined, Blockages

_____

_____

_____

_____

Notes

_____

_____

_____

_____

_____

_____

_____

Three of Wands

Lord of Established Strength. The Three of Wands depicts a man, looking out to sea, resting his hand upon the wand furthest to his right. The Three of Wands is correspondent to the reality of 'me' coming to terms with 'you' and 'I.' While the truth is that, 'you' and 'I.' are interchangeable to 'me' The implicit need for self assertion relies upon the 'I.' to be grounded as consciousness progresses towards the mental reality of the world.

Upright

Strategy, Planning, Strength, Travel, Progression, Expansion, Foresight, Responsibility

_____
_____
_____
_____

Reverse

Delay, Obstacles, Risk, Disappointment, Playing Small, Lack of Foresight, Conceit

_____
_____
_____
_____

Notes

_____
_____
_____
_____
_____
_____
_____
_____

Four of Wands

Lord of Perfected Work. The Four of Wands depicts the creation of elemental form for the figures of sacred masculine and divine feminine to be united within the temple, standing front and center. The Four of Wands shows us we are returning to a state of familiarity, intimacy, openness, and security. It is essential to observe small milestones, showing gratitude for the fruits of labor to be lifted up together.

Upright

Celebration, Community, Joy, Harmony, Relaxation, Homecoming, Success

_____

_____

_____

_____

Reverse

Tension, Instability, Conflict, Insecurity, Unreliability, Anxiety, Insincerity, Delays, Disruption

_____

_____

_____

_____

Notes

_____

_____

_____

_____

_____

_____

_____

_____

Five of Wands

Lord of Strife. The Five of Wands depicts five men swinging their wands at one another as they make attempts to know themselves, creating strife as the resulting projection of discordant chaos implicit to conscious awareness. The Five of Wands is correspondent to the subconscious progression of consciousness as recognition of correspondent reflection of internal and external alignment becomes resolute. This is a glimpse of the lunar body at war within and without, trying to understand being.

Upright

Conflict, Disagreement, Resistance, Competition, Tension, Strife, Struggle, Unrest

_____

_____

_____

_____

Reverse

Resolution, Tension Released, Self-Awareness, Negotiation, Realizations, Peace

_____

_____

_____

_____

Notes

_____

_____

_____

_____

_____

_____

_____

_____

Six of Wands

Lord of Victory. The Six of Wands depicts a man riding a white horse, holding his wand upright; both he and the wand are unified in correspondence, shown with the laurel atop their head. The Six of Wands corresponds with the completion of lunar recognition, as the solar body is found upon further reflection. All the men, who were fighting, are now calm and submissive to the harmony of an expanding understanding of the reality of the world; as above, so below.

Upright

Confidence, Recognition, Progress, Self-Assurance, Conquest, Triumph, Insolence

_____

_____

_____

_____

Reverse

Delay, Fear, Private Achievement, Fall from Grace, Egotism, Doubt, Neglect, Self-Doubt, Uncertainty

_____

_____

_____

_____

Notes

_____

_____

_____

_____

_____

_____

_____

_____

Seven of Wands

Lord of Valour. The Seven of Wands depicts a man on top of a hill wearing two different shoes, armed with a wand, fighting off six more wands drawing up from below. Correspondent with mastery of law, having the strength to move the lower by utilizing the higher. He is entrenched in combat as the totality of lunar and solar conscious awareness comes to a head; reflected with having his feet in both worlds.

Upright

Challenge, Defense, Justification, Competition, Protection, Perseverance, Valor, Advantage

_____
_____
_____
_____

Reverse

Judgment, Weakness, Exhaustion, Ignorance, Pretense, Wrangling Threats

_____
_____
_____
_____

Notes

_____
_____
_____
_____
_____
_____
_____

Eight of Wands

Lord of Swiftness. The Eight of Wands depicts eight sprouting wands soaring through the air in four groups, one of all, one of four, and two of two. The Eight of Wands is correspondent to an expanded state of awareness to the foresight of events in time and the necessity for engagement and action. The continuation of their current mode of being is reliant on the need for order alongside the necessity for change.

Upright

Action, Balance, Change, Productivity, Movement, Fast Paced Change, Alignment

_____

_____

_____

_____

Reverse

Frustration, Delay, Mistakes, Confusion, Resisting Change, Oppression, Dispute, Jealousy

_____

_____

_____

_____

Notes

_____

_____

_____

_____

_____

_____

_____

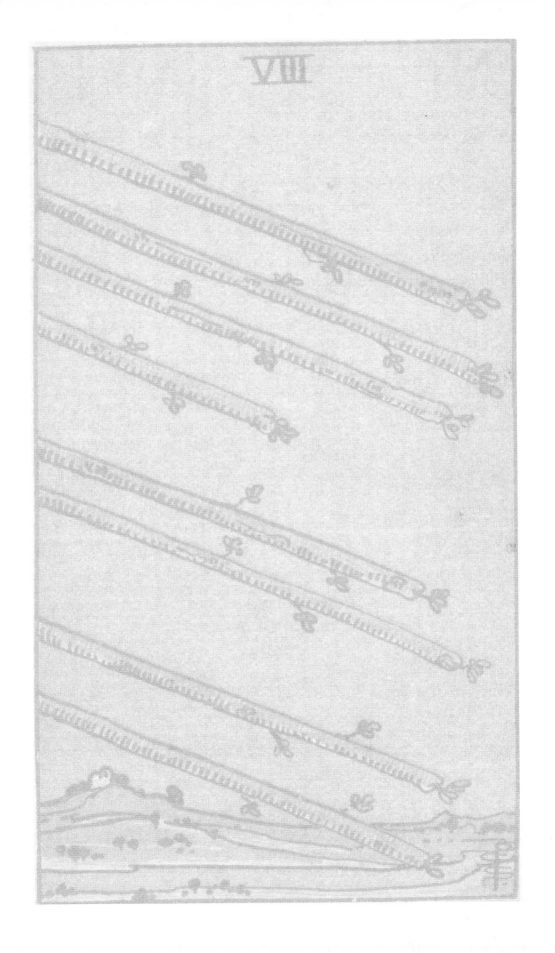

Nine of Wands

Lord of Great Strength. The Nine of Wands depicts an injured man, clutching his wand, while eight wands stand in the background, correspondent to the subconscious flow of being and becoming, providing the stage for the conscious vessel to sail upon unconscious waters. The Ninth wand, held by the injured man, is correspondent to the reality of the in-lighting truth and revelation in being of conscious embrace.

Upright

Courage, Determination, Persistence, Hope, Resilience, Test of Will, Great Success

_____

_____

_____

_____

Reverse

Failure, Insecurity, Hesitation, Paranoia, Struggle, Obstinance, Calamity, Delay, Disaster

_____

_____

_____

_____

Notes

_____

_____

_____

_____

_____

_____

_____

_____

Ten of Wands

Lord of Oppression. The Ten of Wands depicts a man bearing the load of all wands, bundled like sticks, towards a small town in the distance; correspondent to the conscious capacity of responsibility for supporting the natural order of the world. This is the completion of the conscious experience correspondent to the wands, the reality of lunar and solar capacity to responsibly harmonize the entirety of response.

Upright

Burden, Stress, Accomplishment, Extra Responsibility, Hard Work, Completion, Nearing Success

_____

_____

_____

_____

Reverse

Ignorance, Relief, Simplification, Avoidance, Immaturity, Selfishness, Repression

_____

_____

_____

_____

Notes

_____

_____

_____

_____

_____

_____

_____

Suit of Cups

Suit of Cups

The Suit of Cups are correspondent to the outpouring inflow of reality and environmental correspondence of balancing response between reflection and reflex.

As Within, So Without.

The progression of the Cups tells the story of conscious movement through subconscious processes. Their focus is on depicting implications of response and significance of being within the flow of relationship. The Cups act as a guide to understanding the receptive capacity of emotional reflection and the responsibility of such.

The Cups are correspondent to emotions and water; their direction is West; and their astral correspondent is Cancer, Scorpio, and Pisces.

King of Cups

Prince of the Chariot of Waters. The King of Cups, fire of water, holds a scepter in one hand and a chalice in the other, correspondent to the vessel bearing vessel. He wears a golden crown on his head and has a necklace made in the image of a fish, both fish and falcon are conjoined in him, as the father figure to the self; keeping the balancing of subconscious waters by harmonizing mentality and heart, in alignment with compassion.

Upright

Balance, Generosity, Strength, Compassionate, Diplomatic, Wise, Thoughtful, Calm

_____

_____

_____

_____

Reverse

Intolerance, Substance Abuse, Moodiness, Fear, Emotional or Spiritual Manipulation

_____

_____

_____

_____

Notes

_____

_____

_____

_____

_____

_____

_____

_____

KING of CUPS.

Queen of Cups

Queen of the Thrones of Waters. The Queen of Cups, water of water, is beautiful and introspective, holding her holy chalice with support. Below her cup is the Holiest of Holies, in which she herself is divine within divine. She is correspondent to the intuition, creativity, and state of flow achieved within a balanced environment. She is connected to her emotions, realizing they are representational to her being as an extension.

Upright

Protection, Intuition, Unconscious Emotion, Creativity, Compassion, Caring, Intuitive

_____
_____
_____
_____

Reverse

Insecurity, Dishonest, Dissatisfaction, Inconsistency of Honor, Emotional Ignorance

_____
_____
_____
_____

Notes

_____
_____
_____
_____
_____
_____
_____

QUEEN of CUPS.

Knight of Cups

Lord of Waves and Water. The Knight of Cups, air of water, is armored in mental harmony to the natural flow of existence, holding his cup with confidence to ensure it remains. Upon his helm is the mark of angels, just as what are attached to his heel. He is the persistence of water, flowing through the largest mountain. The Knight of Cups is the mental correspondence of emotions as that which progresses through subconscious process, manifest of truth.

Upright

Advancement, Fulfillment, Inspiration, Healing, Creativity, Charm, Beauty, Graceful

_____

_____

_____

_____

Reverse

Boastful, Disappointment, Egotism, Overactive Imagination, Illusion Unnoticed

_____

_____

_____

_____

Notes

KNIGHT of CUPS.

Page of Cups

Princess of the Palace of Floods. The Page of Cups, earth of water, wears a beret and sash on her head, looking like flowing water as she stands near the sea. She upholds her golden cup and her fish companion peaks out his head to observe her. The Page of Cups is the manifest reality of the subconscious processes playing out in physicality. Her appearance is the revelation of circumstantial awareness found in reality of mentalism.

Upright

Confidence, Happiness, Contentment, Insight, Surprise, Opportunity, Intuition, Curiosity

_____

_____

_____

_____

Reverse

Apathy, Impulsiveness, Doubting Intuition, Creative Blocks, Emotional Ignorance

_____

_____

_____

_____

Notes

PAGE of CUPS.

Ace of Cups

Lord of the Root of the Powers of Water. The Ace of Cups depicts a golden hand appearing from without the clouds of unconscious manifestation holding a chalice overflowing in five streams, while the white dove of the Holy Spirit delivers the Eucharist. The Ace of Cups is correspondent to the natural outpouring of the holy spirit, the divine nature of subconscious reality manifest in the being conscious, of such.

Upright

Compassion, Purity, Creativity, Beginnings, Love, Relationships, Abundance, Fertility, Beauty

_____

_____

_____

_____

Reverse

Repressed Emotions, Separation, Vulnerability, Unrequited Love, Intuition Ignored

_____

_____

_____

_____

Notes

_____

_____

_____

_____

_____

_____

_____

ACE of CUPS.

Two of Cups

Lord of Love. The Two of Cups depicts a man and woman, each with cup in hand. The man is reaching toward the woman in the completion of the golden wand of caduceus. This wand is christened with the winged head of Lion, Mithra. The Two of Cups is correspondent to the sacred and divine relationship and significance to the reality of such occasion. Revealing the truth of totality in the spiritual experience of lunar and solar layers of manifestation and relationship.

Upright

Health, Partnership, Harmony, Attraction, Holy Matrimony, Mirth, Reparation, Splendor

_____

_____

_____

_____

Reverse

Imbalance, Disconnection, Unworthiness, Struggle, Folly, Waste, Dissipation, Division

_____

_____

_____

_____

Notes

_____

_____

_____

_____

_____

_____

_____

_____

Three of Cups

Lord of Abundance. The Three of Cups depicts three people dancing in circles, all of them joyfully have their chalice raised high, singing in harmony as the joy of their spirit swirls around them. The Three of Cups is correspondent to the maturity of recognizing individualized consciousness, subconscious progression, and unconsciousness totality; represented in the world of man, being responsibly aligned in love.

Upright

Community, Friendship, Creativity, Collaboration, Fortune, Love, Kindness

_____
_____
_____
_____

Reverse

Over-Indulgence, Unfaithfulness, Stifled Creativity, Disconnection, Isolation, Loss

_____
_____
_____
_____

Notes

_____
_____
_____
_____
_____
_____
_____

Four of Cups

Lord of Blended Pleasure. The Four of Cups depicts the young man in meditation, sitting with his back resting upon a large tree. Before him, three cups are arrayed and the fourth is supported in the air upon the power of aces. The Four of Cups is correspondent to the sacred significance of the becoming oneness of solar consciousness. The selfless affluence of expression, bridging the experience of relationship.

Upright

Meditation, Mentalism, Acknowledgment of Reality, Pursuits, Success, Rejuvenation

_____

_____

_____

_____

Reverse

Withdrawal, Boredom, Inexperience, Depression, Resistance to Disillusionment

_____

_____

_____

_____

Notes

_____

_____

_____

_____

_____

_____

_____

Five of Cups

Lord of Loss in Pleasure. The Five of Cups depicts a man covered by a black cloak, showing a fallen countenance. Before him there are three fallen cups, behind him, there are two cups standing upright. The Five of Cups is correspondent to the assertion of being; it is a conscious choice to accept the reality of what is, with open arms and embrace, undoing the knots and ties of death for life to seed life eternal.

Upright

Loss, Neglect, Despair, Regret, Failure, Disappointment, Death, Sorrow, Treachery, Betrayal

_____
_____
_____
_____

Reverse

Acceptance, Forgiveness, Melancholia, Setbacks, Moving On, Charity, Kindness

_____
_____
_____
_____

Notes

_____
_____
_____
_____
_____
_____
_____

Six of Cups

Lord of Pleasure. The Six of Cups depicts an array of cups full of flowers, while a young boy hands a cup with flowers to the younger girl, who beams with excitement. The Six of Cups is correspondent to the sacred conscious act to assign meaning to the divine feminine form and patterns of force. It is the innocence and purity of healthy and mature awareness to the unconscious significance of the meanings we ascribe to reality.

Upright

Innocence, Nostalgia, Joy, Reunion, Pleasure, Steady and Sustainable Gain

_____

_____

_____

_____

Reverse

Scarcity, Naivete, Abuse, Disappointment, Isolation, Living in the Past, Strife

_____

_____

_____

_____

Notes

Seven of Cups

Lord of Illusionary Success. The Seven of Cups depicts a man standing before seven cups, each filled with value and significance. The Seven of Cups is correspondent to the conscious experiences held within the unconscious field of potential. It is the expanse of opportunity before him, offering the choice of a lifetime. Unbeknownst to him, all cups share a likeness and may be revealed in metamorphosis.

Upright

Illusion, Imagination, Unrealistic Desires, Possibility, Confusion, Opportunities, Choices

_____

_____

_____

_____

Reverse

Temptation, Insecurity, Need for Alignment, Need for a Reevaluation of Values

_____

_____

_____

_____

Notes

_____

_____

_____

_____

_____

_____

_____

Eight of Cups

Lord of Abandoned Success. The Eight of Cups depicts a man climbing the embankment with his cane, beginning his long walk upon the trail stretching into the further reaches of the horizon, illuminated by the moon. The Eight of Cups is correspondent to feelings of isolation in light of lunar consciousness. The revelation appears as personal experience of self prior to the appearance of solar conscious reality.

Upright

Abandonment, Isolation, Loss of Interest, Withdrawal, Journey's Closing, Weakness of Resolve

_____

_____

_____

_____

Reverse

Confusion, Drifting, Rejection, Happiness, Festivity, Joy, Indecision, Aimlessness, Anxiety

_____

_____

_____

_____

Notes

_____

_____

_____

_____

_____

_____

_____

_____

Nine of Cups

Lord of Material Happiness. The Nine of Cups depicts a man seated with his arms crossed in pride, with nine cups in display behind him. The Nine of Cups is correspondent to the totality of lunar fruition, mimicking the brilliance of the solar consciousness. It is the attraction of material being in extension of becoming, the totality of all which could manifest with correspondent conscious action and will to manifest.

Upright

Contentment, Gratitude, Wishes Come True, Ambitions Fulfilled, Extensive Expression of Desires

_____

_____

_____

_____

Reverse

Greed, Unrealistic Expectations, Boastfulness, Dissatisfaction, Indulgence, Hedonism, Gluttony

_____

_____

_____

_____

Notes

_____

_____

_____

_____

_____

_____

_____

Ten of Cups

Lord of Perfected Success. The Ten of Cups depicts a happy family, frolicking beneath a rainbow, showcasing the fruits of marriage. The Ten of Cups are correspondent to the truth of value and success in the sustainable. It's the actualization of solar consciousness, the sacred masculine and divine feminine oneness bringing fruition to intent, as their actions are celebrated in the sky with the light of grounded with joy.

Upright

Abundance, Sacred and Divine Love, Fulfillment, Happiness, Bliss, Harmony, Alignment

_____

_____

_____

_____

Reverse

Broken Trust, Neglect, Misalignment, Tragedy, Shattered Dreams

_____

_____

_____

_____

Notes

Suit of Swords

Suit of Swords

The Suit of Swords are correspondent to the mentalism associated with the conscious reality of belief, understanding, and the assertion of perspective experience.

The progression of the Swords tells the story of the individual experience of environmental engagement. Their focus is on depicting the reality of growth and maturity as the responsibility of familiar relationship is upheld. They act as the conscious guide through the subconscious process of realizing internal and external alignment and the realization of such acknowledgments.

The Swords are correspondent to mentalism and air; their direction is North; and their astral correspondence is Gemini, Libra, and Aquarius.

King of Swords

Prince of the Chariots of the Winds. The King of Swords, fire of air, depicts a king sitting on a throne butterflies. Holding his sword carefully, he rests his left hand on his lap. The King of Swords is correspondent with the resolute force of action. He is the mental capacity to shift contextual perspective awareness to adapt alongside the progressing reality of life. The King of Swords is the shrewd and observant perception to see through the illusion of falsehood and deceit.

Upright

Intellect, Authority, Strength, Mental Clarity, Thought, Distrust, Caution, Suspicion

_____
_____
_____
_____

Reverse

Malicious, Indecision, Cruel, Abusive, Manipulative, Hesitant, Sadistic, Unreliable, Harsh

_____
_____
_____
_____

Notes

_____
_____
_____
_____
_____
_____
_____
_____

KING of SWORDS.

Queen of Swords

Queen of the Thrones of Air. The Queen of Swords, water of air, depicts a queen wearing a crown of butterflies. Holding her sword firmly she motions with her left hand. Upon her cloak are clouds, correspondent to the divine capacity for divine revelation as the clouds part for the truth to be revealed by the eyes who acknowledge. The Queen of Swords is the divine form of revelatory forces of truth.

Upright

Confidence, Assurance, Intellect, Independence, Unbiased Judgment, Communication

_____

_____

_____

_____

Reverse

Cruel, Distant, Emotional, Easily Influenced, Cold-Hearted, Sly, Foxy, Unreliable, Deceitful

_____

_____

_____

_____

Notes

_____

_____

_____

_____

_____

_____

_____

_____

QUEEN of SWORDS.

Knight of Swords

Lord of the Winds and Breezes. The Knight of Swords, air of air, depicts a knight charging forth upon an anxious white horse. The Knight of Swords corresponds to the expansive and adaptive capacity of mental awareness and perspective. He is the assurance to act with a resolute heart. He is the reflective force of energy and mental resilience to address issues as they arise, properly handling each while adapting on the fly.

Upright

Stubborn, Determined, Ambitious, Action-Oriented, Inclination, Resolve, Courage

_____

_____

_____

_____

Reverse

Weak, Unreliable, Disorganized, Restless, Unfocused, Impulsive, Tyrannical, Disunion

_____

_____

_____

_____

Notes

_____

_____

_____

_____

_____

_____

_____

KNIGHT of SWORDS .

Page of Swords

Princess of the Rushing Winds. The Page of Swords, earth of air, depicts a princess stanced, holding her sword up high, while her hair flows in the wind. The Page of Swords is correspondent to the mental extension of earth stretching into manifest correspondence of with existence. She is the fact of the matter inspiring the idea of ascribed significance implicit to the being of extension into physical manifestation.

Upright

Thoughtfulness, Clarity, Curiosity, New Ideas, Wisdom, Acuteness, Grace, Vigilance

_____

_____

_____

_____

Reverse

Irritable, Hasty, Doubtful, Frivolous, Cunning, Illness, Delayed Projects, Indecision

_____

_____

_____

_____

Notes

_____

_____

_____

_____

_____

_____

_____

PAGE of SWORDS.

Ace of Swords

Lord of the Root of the Powers of Air. The Ace of Swords depicts a golden hand appearing from without the clouds of unconscious manifestation, baring a sword held upright. It is moving through the bottom of the crown, with garlands draping over. The Ace of Swords is correspondent to the manifestation of consciousness break through the subconscious realities of the spiritual existence of mentalism.

Upright

Focus, Clarity, Inspiration, Breakthrough, Invocation of Power, Justice, Success

_____
_____
_____
_____

Reverse

Insecurity, Confusion, Boredom, Debacle, Tyranny, Self-Destruction, Disaster

_____
_____
_____
_____

Notes

_____
_____
_____
_____
_____
_____
_____

ACE of SWORDS.

Two of Swords

Lord of Peace Restored. The Two of Swords depicts a blindfolded woman, dressed in a white robe, holding two crossed swords. The Two of Swords is correspondent with intimations of intuitive assurance, the knowing of mentalism; further established by the crescent moon hanging in the distance. The swords she holds are in perfect balance as an extension of her, the balance of intelligence with intuition.

Upright

Intuition, Compromise, Balanced Force, Peace Restored, Harmony, Inner Peace, Stable Mentalism

_____

_____

_____

_____

Reverse

Fear, Confusion, Duplicity, Falsehood, Misrepresentation, Illusion Seeking

_____

_____

_____

_____

Notes

Three of Swords

Lord of Sorrow. The Three of Swords depicts three swords piercing through a heart, falling from clouds like rain, anchoring the heart down as they cross within the flesh. The Three of Swords corresponds with the mental capacity to receive the intimations of guidance, which may manifest in varying degrees of significance and relevance.

Upright

Pain, Grief, Deception, Rejection, Separation, Strife, Mischief, Discord, Faithfulness in Promise

_____

_____

_____

_____

Reverse

Introspection, Alienation, Insecurity, Mental Affliction, Emotional Repression

_____

_____

_____

_____

Notes

_____

_____

_____

_____

_____

_____

_____

_____

Four of Swords

Lord of Rest from Strife. The Four of Swords depicts the grave of a knight in full armor. Three swords, pointing downward, indicative of his resolve to remain in attendance of the guard which lead to his rest. Engraved onto his coffin, is a sword laying parallel to him. The Four of Swords is correspondent to the relief of the hunter, upon revelation of his savior.

Upright

Contemplation, Meditation, Relaxation, Rest After Strife, Abundance, Respite, Peace

_____

_____

_____

_____

Reverse

Resentment, Exhaustion, Self-Seeking, Frustration, Not Knowing When to Stop or Rest

_____

_____

_____

_____

Notes

_____

_____

_____

_____

_____

_____

_____

Five of Swords

Lord of Defeat. The Five of Swords depicts a man standing tall, holding two swords in his left hand and planting one with his right, and his hair is red and fierce. The Five of Swords is correspondent to the self-seeker, the vampirical abuser of substance, tireless rabbit hole invader. It is the conscious pursuit of the divine for the simple thrill of the chase, the endless desire to chase the dragon of eternal illusion.

Upright

Selfishness, Tension, Betrayal, Entitlement, Failure, Contests Finished with Disappointment

_____

_____

_____

_____

Reverse

Resolution, Forgiveness, Understanding, Turning a New Leaf, Weakness Tested

_____

_____

_____

_____

Notes

_____

_____

_____

_____

_____

_____

_____

_____

Six of Swords

Lord of Earned Success. The Six of Swords depicts a man at the rear of a boat, crossing the water to ferry a mother and her child, with six swords at the helm. The Six of Swords corresponds with the vessel bearing vessel, the conscious solar barge transporting the child and his mother across the subconscious flow of the correspondent unconsciousness.

Upright

Solutions, Change, Security, Transition, Dominion, Labor, Movement into the Unknown

_____
_____
_____
_____

Reverse

Delay, Procrastination, Stalemate, Unwanted Proposal, Mental Fog, Directionless

_____
_____
_____
_____

Notes

_____
_____
_____
_____
_____
_____
_____
_____

Seven of Swords

Lord of Unstable Effort. The Seven of Swords depicts a man sneaking away with a bundle of five swords, behind him two swords are planted to his rear. In the distance, there is a military encampment, showing us where the man likely stole these items. The Seven of Swords is correspondent to the adoption of unearned knowledge and burglary of innovative ideas and unoriginal ideologies.

Upright

Betrayal, Deception, Theft, Irresponsibility, Partial Success, Yielding to Victory, Subterfuge

_____

_____

_____

_____

Reverse

Responsibility, Acceptance, Challenges, Commitment, Self-Deceit, Illusionary Bias, Shame

_____

_____

_____

_____

Notes

_____

_____

_____

_____

_____

_____

_____

_____

Eight of Swords

Lord of Shortened Force. The Eight of Swords depicts a woman bound and blindfolded with eight swords surrounding her. At her feet is a pool of water; suggesting, although she is bound and blinded, she can trust what she feels. She need only release the limiting beliefs which bind her, her suffering is related to her journey in life, bound up and surrounded by swords on all sides; yet, at her feet, she can feel the truth of waters edge.

Upright

Isolation, Disappointment,
Entrapment by Illusion,
Excessive Force Hastily Applied

_____
_____
_____
_____

Reverse

Release, Acceptance,
Accountability, Discovery,
Difficulty, High Openness

_____
_____
_____
_____

Notes

_____
_____
_____
_____
_____
_____
_____
_____

Nine of Swords

Lord of Despair and Cruelty. The Nine of Swords depicts a woman tormented by the projections of her psyche. Clutching her face, she is tormented by inability to accept the sacred projections upon the divine feminine blanket of space. Her perceived resentment of existential significance is shown in her fear of the swords pointing forward.

Upright

Depression, Crisis, Fear, Anxiety, Despair, Suffering, Lying, Dishonesty, Despondency

_____
_____
_____
_____

Reverse

Objectivity, Perception, Recovery, Revelation, Doubt, Suspicion, Timidity, Resolution

_____
_____
_____
_____

Notes

_____
_____
_____
_____
_____
_____
_____

Ten of Swords

Lord of Ruin. The Ten of Swords depicts a man stabbed in the back with ten swords, grounding him in revelation of truth. The Ten of Swords is correspondent to the idea's, mentalities, and thoughts culminating into the penultimate revelation of being. Embracing reality ensures a smooth transition into awareness, realizing the truth through the subconscious process of the truth function, is self-centered betrayal.

Upright

Endings, Betrayal, Surrender, Defeat, Wounds, Disruption, Failure, Resisting Inevitable Ends

_____

_____

_____

_____

Reverse

Hope, Recovery, Acceptance, Renewal, Clever, Cute, Beneficial, Transformation

_____

_____

_____

_____

Notes

_____

_____

_____

_____

_____

_____

_____

_____

Suit of Pentacles

Suit of Pentacles

The Suit of Pentacles are correspondent to the divine extension of mental significance to recieve the sacred outpouring of consciousness.

The progression of the Pentacles tells the story of the conscious environment as an extension of the sacred and divine relation of significance. Their focus is on depicting the correspondence of conscious responsibility through an environment of subconscious regard. They act as a guide to the reality of environmental communication between sacred and divine. Providing insight to the relevancy of significance communicative intent has upon the reality of expression.

The Pentacles are correspondent to the correspondence of being and Earth; their direction is East; and their astral correspondence is Taurus, Virgo, and Capricorn.

King of Pentacles

Prince of the Chariot of Earth. The King of Pentacles, fire of earth, sits with his left hand upon the pentacle and his right hand holding his wand. The King of Pentacles is correspondent to figure of abundance and prosperity. Understanding the reality of nature and the phenomenal experience of an ordered existence, the King of Pentacles is the practical application and extension of will, within matters of significance.

Upright

Power, Influence, Strength, Abundance, Character, Intelligence, Practicality

_____

_____

_____

_____

Reverse

Substance Abuse, Suppression, Instability, Luciferianism, Stupidity, Corruption, Stubborn

_____

_____

_____

_____

Notes

_____

_____

_____

_____

_____

_____

_____

KING of PENTACLES.

Queen of Pentacles

Queen of the Thrones of Earth. The Queen of Pentacles, water of earth, sits with her hands supporting the golden pentacle. She is dressed in brightly colored robes, with a headdress being one with the very source of nature itself. The Queen of Pentacles is correspondent with the divine significance of woman divine, the abundance of nature, rich in prosperity and potential.

Upright

Prosperity, Pleasure, Motherly, Security, Charming, Intelligent, Kind, Truthful, Practical

_____

_____

_____

_____

Reverse

Imbalance, Reclusive, Superficial, Capricious, Foolish, False Prosperity, Changeable

_____

_____

_____

_____

Notes

QUEEN of PENTACLES

Knight of Pentacles

Lord of the Wild and Fertile Land. The Knight of Pentacles, air of earth, wearing his suit of armor, upon his massive black horse, he upholds the pentacle. The Knight of Pentacles is correspondent to the solar conscious reality of our existential armor being the lunar conscious expression of our being. It is the reflection and extension projected in outward fashion, manifest in the physicality of the life we pursue and horse we ride.

Upright

Prepared, Efficient, Ambitious, Practical, Methodical, Magnetic, Productive, Persistent

_____

_____

_____

_____

Reverse

Stagnant, Lazy, Careless, Idle, Boredom, Feeling 'Stuck', Perfectionism, Insecurity

_____

_____

_____

_____

Notes

_____

_____

_____

_____

_____

_____

_____

_____

KNIGHT of PENTACLES.

Page of Pentacles

Princess of the Echoing Hills. The Page of Pentacles, earth of earth, is the woman in appreciative contemplation over the pentacle in her hand. Wearing a hat, similar to the Page of Cups, the Page of Pentacles realizes the truth of her 'fish', being the pentacle, who is she. The Page of Pentacles corresponds to the reality of existential extensions of phenomenality within the physicality of our being, within and without.

Upright

Opportunity, Discovery, Manifestation, Mastery, Kind, Generous, Diligence, Prudence

_____

_____

_____

_____

Reverse

Ignorance, Immaturity, Resentment, Wasteful, Dissipation of Ideas, Unrealistic

_____

_____

_____

_____

Notes

_____

_____

_____

_____

_____

_____

_____

_____

PAGE of PENTACLES.

Ace of Pentacles

Lord of the Root of the Powers of Earth. The Ace of Pentacles depicts the golden hand, manifest from without the clouds, supporting a golden pentacle. The Ace of Pentacles corresponds to being, in and of itself, within the all of all. The significance is manifest within is the garden of lilies, enclosed within the hedge; where, through the archway, two mountains are seen, projecting the truth of the garden, within the garden. As well as the significance of such valuable truth, being in and of itself.

Upright

Prosperity, Stability, New Beginnings, Maturity, Abundance and Illusion

_____

_____

_____

_____

Reverse

Greed, Corruption, Risk, Delay, Prosperity without Joy, Misused Wealth, Lack of Foresight

_____

_____

_____

_____

Notes

_____

_____

_____

_____

_____

_____

_____

Two of Pentacles

Lord of Harmonious Change. The Two of Pentacles depicts the woman dancing along the flow of the universe holding two pentacles; while in the distance, seafaring vessels sail along the ups and downs. The Two of Pentacles corresponds with the karmic flow of reason and causality. It is significant to the affect of magnetism and law alongside the physical extension and inspiration of such ideas.

Upright

Balanced, Renewal, Adaptability, The Harmony of Change, Correspondence Reflex

_____

_____

_____

_____

Reverse

Forced Gaiety, Inflexibility, Irresponsibility, Neglect, Unpredictability, Discord

_____

_____

_____

_____

Notes

_____

_____

_____

_____

_____

_____

_____

Three of Pentacles

Lord of Material Work. The Three of Pentacles depicts three people, beneath the masculine triangle of three pentacles conjoined of the Earth, over the feminine triangle of blossoming earth. The Three of Pentacles corresponds with the harmony of collaborative interplay; the master who holds the hammer, the priest who divines the significance, and the modest woman who bares the blueprints of the castle.

Upright

Success, Collaboration, Confidence, Constructive Force, Great Skill in Trade or Work

_____
_____
_____
_____

Reverse

Competition, Interference, Low Quality, Mediocrity, Preoccupation, Sloppiness

_____
_____
_____
_____

Notes

_____
_____
_____
_____
_____
_____
_____
_____

Four of Pentacles

Lord of Earthly Power. The Four of Pentacles depicts a woman with her feet planted firmly upon two pentacles, while clutching a third around her heart, supporting the fourth with the crown above her head. The Four of Pentacles corresponds with the stability of knowing her feet stand upon the protection of her heart, supported by the spirit above her crown.

Upright

Stability, Control, Influence, Security, Success and Gain, Power, Integration, Careful

_____

_____

_____

_____

Reverse

Greed, Loss, Materialism, Mistrust, Obstacles, Lack of Originality, Prejudice, Setbacks

_____

_____

_____

_____

Notes

_____

_____

_____

_____

_____

_____

_____

Five of Pentacles

Lord of Material Trouble. The Five of Pentacles depicts a woman clutching her cloak while an injured man hobbles behind her. They are walking in the snow storm outside of a temple adorned with an image of a tree with five pentacles in apex. The Five of Pentacles corresponds with the reality of consciousness to be responsible for the matters of significance in full view, to embrace the labors of life with vigilant awareness and love.

Upright

Isolation, Poverty, Poor Health, Toil, Labor, Cultivation, Knowledge, Acuteness

_____

_____

_____

_____

Reverse

Financial Recovery, Renewed Confidence, Opportunity, Determination, Sanctuary

_____

_____

_____

_____

Notes

Six of Pentacles

Lord of Material Success. The Six of Pentacles depicts a man dressed in many layers, blessing an injured man with his right hand, upholding the balance of divine scales in his left. The Six of Pentacles corresponds with the significance of solar responsibility to bare justice accordingly to the precepts of your soul. To deal with all, according to their own, within the context of their being and the actions of their becoming.

Upright

Generosity, Charity, Empathy, Kindness, Union of the Sacred and Divine, Appropriation

_____
_____
_____
_____

Reverse

Selfishness, Greed, Cruelty, Judgment, Medusian Complex, Vampiricism, Satanism

_____
_____
_____
_____

Notes

_____
_____
_____
_____
_____
_____
_____

Seven of Pentacles

Lord of Success Unfulfilled. The Seven of Pentacles depicts a man observing the fruits of his effort ripening upon the vine while supporting his head with his hoe. The Seven of Pentacles corresponds with ignorance to the significance of intent as the inspired extension to labor, stretching into affect implication of the laborer, as an existential extension of being.

Upright

Profit, Hopes Deceived and Crushed, Forging the Stairway to Heaven, Delay in Profit

_____

_____

_____

_____

Reverse

Failure, Mistrust, Impatience, Uneasiness, Anxiety, Slave Master Mentality

_____

_____

_____

_____

Notes

Eight of Pentacles

Lord of Prudence. The Eight of Pentacles depicts a man dutifully working away at his craft. Using chisel and hammer, he forges his eighth pentacle. The Eight of Pentacles corresponds with the inspired action following the acknowledgment of intent and application of force as significant to the affect of existential extension, correspondent reflex manifestation.

Upright

Creativity, Craftsmanship, Focus, Apprenticeships, Forging Divine Principal Interest

_____

_____

_____

_____

Reverse

Frustration, Setbacks, Obsession, Avarice, Industriousness, Hoarding, Poor Effort

_____

_____

_____

_____

Notes

_____

_____

_____

_____

_____

_____

_____

_____

Nine of Pentacles

Lord of Material Gain. The Nine of Pentacles depicts a woman as she places her right hand upon the fruit of her pentacle while a falcon, wearing blinders, is perched on her hand. The Nine of Pentacles corresponds to the prosperity and abundance of solar consciousness in correspondence to the reality that "I." and "You" are one and the same. The inspired extension of significance portrayed in the Eight of Pentacles.

Upright

Luxury, Success, Reward, Appreciation, Abundance, Complete Integration of Reality

_____

_____

_____

_____

Reverse

Setbacks, Loss, Theft, Knavery, Dissipation, Bad Faith, Danger, Loss of Independence

_____

_____

_____

_____

Notes

_____

_____

_____

_____

_____

_____

_____

_____

Ten of Pentacles

Lord of Wealth. The Ten of Pentacles depicts a man with white hair and a golden blonde beard, extending his hand to pet the head of a dog. In the distance, there is a man and woman speaking to one another, while a child pets the tail of another dog. The Ten of Pentacles corresponds to the intercontextual oneness of reality; whereby the environment surrounding us corresponds to the expression and extension of our being, as one.

Upright

Wealth, Family, Pinnacle of Success, The Divine Romance, Holy Union, Pearl Retrieved

_____
_____
_____
_____

Reverse

Burden, Loss, Judgment, Luciferianism, Old Age, Great Wealth Yet Feelings of Emptiness

_____
_____
_____
_____

Notes

_____
_____
_____
_____
_____
_____
_____
_____

Thanks for your purchase!

Be sure to stay tuned in for future updates and learn how you can turn your pictures into cards to have your very own personalized deck!

Don't forget to share your art at
#WithinTheLines

Made in the USA
Columbia, SC
05 February 2022